ASIAN MAMMALS

written and illustrated by
JOHN LEIGH-PEMBERTON

Publishers : Ladybird Books Ltd . Loughborough
© Ladybird Books Ltd (formerly Wills & Hepworth Ltd) 1971
Printed in England

Tarsier (*centre left*)	Length, head and body	14 cm.
	Length, tail	20 cm.
Slow Loris (*top right*)	Length, head and body	34 cm.
Oriental Pygmy Squirrel (*lower right*)	Length, head and body	9.5 cm.
	Length, tail	6.5 cm.

The huge eyes of the Tarsier (family *Tarsidae*) indicate that it is a nocturnal animal, while the fingered hands and feet with their soft pads indicate that it is also arboreal.* The head can be rotated through almost 360° and the movements when climbing or on the ground are almost frog-like. Tarsiers are insectivorous, and produce one young at a time, each fairly well developed, fully furred and with eyes open. There is no nest, the young being carried about by the mother, either clinging to her fur or held by her mouth.

Tarsiers are one of the most ancient of all Primates and are found in Sumatra, Java, Borneo and the Philippines.

From the same region comes another Primate, the Slow Loris, (family *Lorisidae*) which also occurs in various forms on the mainland of Asia. This is another nocturnal animal which moves about cautiously, hunting for insects, fruit and small mammals. The young are born singly and are carried by the mother until almost fully grown.

Both Tarsiers and Lorises emit twittering, bird-like cries and, in spite of their mild appearance, will bite hard if frightened.

Asia contains both the largest (the Giant Indian Squirrel) and the smallest Squirrels known. The smallest is the Oriental Pygmy Squirrel (order *Rodentia*, family *Sciuridae*), five species of which are found in Java, Borneo, Sumatra and the Philippines. Beautifully marked, they occur in a variety of colours and patterns. They are primarily vegetarian and diurnal.* They are believed to produce three or four young in each litter and there may be more than one litter a year.

* arboreal—live in trees
* diurnal—active in the daytime

0 7214 0290 9

The huge and ancient continent of Asia extends from the Arctic pack-ice to the Equator and beyond, and from the Mediterranean to the Pacific. It contains huge areas of desert, vast tracts of jungle, the expanse of the steppes and forests, great ranges of mountains which include the highest points on the globe, and countless islands. In this great variety of habitats lives a mammal population of enormous diversity and of great age. For it was probably in this region that the mammals first took over from the reptiles and began to dominate the earth as they spread outwards into Europe and Africa and across the land bridge to America.

We probably know less about the Asian mammals than we do of those of Africa or America. The reason lies in the fact that often the terrain is so isolated and inaccessible, shut off from exploration by huge distances, by mountain and desert barriers which seem impassable, and by impenetrable jungle. Moreover, many Asian mammals, hiding in dense vegetation, are also nocturnal and are thus rarely seen.

To-day, the prospect for Asian mammals is somewhat depressing. In much of Asia, human populations are expanding at an enormous rate. The demand for new areas for human living space and agriculture is increasingly insistent. Other species, large and small, are being subjected to pressures so great that all our efforts will be required to ensure their survival.

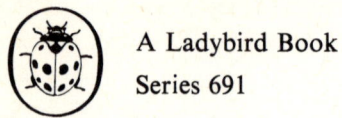

A Ladybird Book
Series 691

'*Asian Mammals*' *is the fifth of a
Ladybird series of books about animals of
the world. The superb full-colour illustrations
by John Leigh-Pemberton, the well known
bird and animal painter, are supported by an
informative text, and a colourful end-paper
shows the various types of habitat of the
animals. An index is given and also, at
the back, a chart showing the various Orders
and Families to which the animals belong.*

Rhesus Macaque (top left)	Length, head and body	50 cm.
	Length, tail	40 cm.
Douc Langur (lower left)	Length, head and body	75 cm.
	Length, tail	60 cm.
Gibbon (centre right)	Length, head and body	55 cm.

There are about thirty species of monkeys in Asia, ranging from Japan to south-west Asia. One of the commonest is the Rhesus Macaque, found in India and southern Asia. This Primate belongs to the family *Cercopithecidae* or Old World Monkeys and is extensively used in medical research. Like most monkeys, Macaques are chiefly vegetarian but also eat some animal food. They are diurnal (active during the day) living in organised groups of about twenty members, and are equally at home on the ground or in the trees. One young a year is normal, but twins are occasionally born. Like all monkeys they make most unsatisfactory pets, becoming unreliable and vicious as they mature.

Also from south Asia (Indo-China) comes the brightly coloured and handsome Douc Langur (family *Cercopithecidae*). Little is known about it and it is unfortunately becoming rare. Other types of Langur, which are long-tailed, leaf-eating monkeys with slender bodies and hands, are found in China, India, Indo-China and Indonesia, usually inhabiting the trees in forest areas. The recently discovered Golden Langur lives in the foothills of the Himalayas, and troupes of Langurs have been observed in the snow.

Gibbons (family *Pongidae*), of which there are about six species, are found in various forms from Assam and Burma to Borneo. These Apes inhabit forests and are the most agile of all tree-dwellers. Small groups or family parties of Gibbons establish their own territory, warning off intruders with loud howling cries. They are principally vegetarian. Female Gibbons carry about their single youngster, which takes almost ten years to mature.

Orang-Utan (*below*)

Length, head and body	140 cm.
Arm spread	225 cm.
Average weight (*male*)	75 Kg.

Banded Linsang
(*above*)

Length, head and body	40 cm.
Length, tail	35 cm.

The Primate family *Pongidae* contains, besides the Gibbons, the Gorillas, Chimpanzees and Orang-Utans, which are known as the Great Apes. Of these the Asian representative is the Orang-Utan (meaning 'Wild Man') which is a native of the forests of Borneo and Sumatra. Existing almost entirely in the trees, Orangs build platform nests, as other Great Apes do, and live in small family parties. In temperament they are normally placid and inquisitive, but can be dangerous if alarmed or molested. When young they are shy but intelligent. Fruit is the main item of a diet which also includes leaves, eggs and young birds.

As they grow older Orangs become grotesque, developing gigantic folds of tissue round the face, and there is great variety in the form this development takes; at times it is remarkably human. The very attractive young are born singly, maturing in about ten years.

Many of these Apes are illegally captured when young to supply the senseless demand for menagerie specimens and pets. The great majority of these die and many adults are slaughtered in the capturing process. Thus, in spite of protection, the Orang-Utan is becoming extremely rare.

Asia has about twenty-five species of small carnivores of the family *Viverridae*, which includes the Civets, Mongooses, Genets and Linsangs. Most of them are nocturnal jungle dwellers, equally at home on the ground or in the trees.

The beautiful Banded Linsang is a graceful little animal found in Malaya, Borneo and Sumatra, while the closely related Spotted Linsang is found on the Asian mainland. Two or three young are produced in two litters each year.

Rasse (Lesser Oriental Civet) *(below)*	Length, head and body	55 cm.
	Length, tail	40 cm.
Dhole *(above)*	Length, head and body	85 cm.
	Length, tail	38 cm.

Another small carnivore which belongs to the family *Viverridae* is the Rasse, a smaller relation of the Oriental Civet. Most members of this family possess glands which produce a powerfully scented substance, often highly offensive, which is used partly as a means of identification and partly as a form of defence. This substance is used in eastern countries as a 'fixative' for perfumes, for medicinal purposes and for flavouring tobacco; and Rasses are kept by natives especially for this purpose, for which Civets have been introduced into parts of the world outside Asia.

Rasses live mostly on the ground in forested areas from China and India to Java and Bali; they are active by both day and night and produce from two to five young, furred but with closed eyes. As well as small mammals they eat carrion and some vegetable food.

The Dhole (family *Canidae*), often inaccurately referred to as the 'Indian Wild Dog', is found in various forms from Russia to Java (but not in Ceylon), usually in wooded regions. These animals (which are not related to Domestic Dogs) live and hunt in packs, rather in the manner of the African Hunting Dog.* They are quite fearless and untameable and packs have been known to attack and kill even a Tiger. No prey, even Buffalo, is too big for them, and they quickly clear an area of all game wherever they occur. They do not attack humans.

Active by both day and night, these carnivores produce from two to six puppies to a litter. They are becoming increasingly rare throughout their extensive range.

*See 'African Mammals' *in this series*

Masked Palm Civet (*above*)	Length, head and body	70 cm.
	Length, tail	60 cm.
Mongoose (*centre*)	Length, head and body	35 cm.
	Length, tail	30 cm.
Ratel (*below*)	Length, head and body	70 cm.
	Length, tail	25 cm.

Palm Civets (family *Viverridae*, order *Carnivora*) are found in one species in Africa as well as in about eight species in Asia. The Masked Palm Civet is found from China to Borneo and in Formosa and Hainan. Particularly potent scent glands are used by this species as a means of defence, and it is arboreal and omnivorous. It is often found living in the dense tops of Palm trees—hence its name. Like all Civets it has retractile claws.

Several species of Mongoose (plural, Mongooses) are found in Madagascar, some thirty more in Africa, and about ten in Asia. Although members of the family *Viverridae*, they do not have retractile claws and some have no scent glands. They are active and often destructive animals, but many have been successfully kept as pets. They are omnivorous, and have a reputation for killing snakes, although they are not immune to snake venom. From two to four young are born in each litter.

The Ratel belongs to the family *Mustelidae* and is sometimes referred to as the Honey Badger, due to its great liking for eating the honey and grubs of wild bees. In this it is assisted (at least in Africa) by a small bird, the Honey Guide, which locates the bees' nest and guides the Ratel to it, sharing the feast.

These carnivores are found in varying habitats in Africa as well as in Asia. They are formidable animals which seem to enjoy fighting, and are so muscular and have a skin so thick and loose that it is almost impossible to hurt them. They are omnivorous and produce two young in each litter.

Sloth Bear (*above*)

Length, head and body	160 cm.
Shoulder height	75 cm.

Muntjac (*below*)

Length, head and body	90 cm.
Length, tail	15 cm.
Shoulder height	50 cm.

There are four species of Bear (family *Ursidae*, order *Carnivora*) found in Asia. These are the Asiatic Black Bear, the Sun Bear, the Sloth Bear and the Brown Bear which also occurs in America and Europe.

The Sloth Bear lives in the forests of India and Ceylon. It is nocturnal and omnivorous and, although quite a dangerous animal, is not strictly carnivorous at all. Its method of eating insects such as bees and termites is peculiar (and very noisy). It opens up the nest, shuts its nostrils, inserts its specially adapted snout and sucks the grubs into its mouth. Two teeth are missing from its upper jaw to make this process easier. The whole procedure is somewhat like the operation of a vacuum cleaner.

Normally slow and sleepy, Sloth Bears can move surprisingly quickly and are expert climbers. Litters consist of from one to three cubs which often ride on the mother's back.

Several species of Muntjac (order *Artiodactyla*, family *Cervidae*) are found in China, India, Java, Borneo and adjacent islands. These dainty little deer, which are chiefly nocturnal and solitary, normally live in forests among thick cover, for they are extremely shy animals, much preyed upon by Leopards and Tigers.

Only the males grow the curious little antlers, which are carried on long, bony ridges or 'pedicels'. Both sexes have canine teeth elongated into tusks with which they can defend themselves effectively against enemies. Muntjac, which have been introduced into some European countries, utter a characteristic bark, usually as an alarm signal. One or two young are born, hidden in dense undergrowth.

Malay Chevrotain (*below*)	Length, head and body	50 cm.
	Length, tail	6 cm.
	Shoulder height	28 cm.
Sun Bear (*above*)	Length, head and body	120 cm.
	Shoulder height	70 cm.

Although Chevrotains (family *Tragulidae*) are sometimes referred to as 'Mouse Deer', they are not closely related to Deer at all, but are more nearly related to the Camels or even Pigs. They have no antlers, but grow canine teeth which form small tusks. They are 'ruminants', which means that, like other members of the order *Artiodactyla*, they 'chew the cud', but have only three stomach compartments instead of the usual four. One Chevrotain species occurs in Africa, while in Asia there are six, found in India, south-east Asia and the East Indies.

Shy, nocturnal, vegetarian and solitary, these little animals form tunnels through dense jungle vegetation, preferring habitats near water. They are much preyed upon by carnivores and by snakes, and also by natives for food. Young are born singly, hidden among dense undergrowth or in a rock crevice.

The Sun Bear (family *Ursidae*), inhabiting mountain and lowland forest in the tropical parts of Asia, is found in Burma and Indo-China as well as in Sumatra, Borneo and Malaya. This is the smallest Bear and is omnivorous, eating anything from birds and small rodents to fruit and insects, but especially honey. Long claws enable it to dig and climb, often to considerable heights, and it spends much time in the trees, where it builds a nest for sleeping during the day. The two cubs, however, are born on the ground.

Of all Bears this is probably the most intelligent, but it is warier than other species. Although many young ones are kept as pets, they quickly become destructive and dangerous when mature.

Musk Deer (*above*)	Length, head and body	100 cm.
	Shoulder height	55 cm.
	Rump height	60 cm.
Lesser Panda (*below*)	Length, head and body	60 cm.
	Length, tail	40 cm.

Musk Deer (family *Cervidae*, order *Artiodactyla*) live in high forest and mountainous areas of northern and central Asia. Their range was once much wider but is now very restricted, as this animal has a gland in its skin which contains 'musk', a substance much used in the manufacture of perfume. As a result the Musk Deer has been hunted almost to extinction throughout the more accessible parts of its range.

These deer, placed in a sub-family (*Moschinae*) by them-selves, have no antlers and no tail, but grow small tusks in the upper jaw. Musk Deer are solitary creatures, and in some ways rather like a Hare*, for they sleep in a 'form' or nest during the day and are vegetarian and timid. The spotted young are usually born singly and, like their mothers, do not produce 'musk', which is found in the adult male only.

From the same area and the same habitat comes the Lesser Panda, a most attractive member of the Raccoon family (*Procyonidae*). Although classed as a carnivore this animal is almost entirely vegetarian, living largely on bam-boo shoots and other vegetation, but occasionally eating birds and their eggs. Largely nocturnal and arboreal, Lesser Pandas live in family groups, and from one to four (usually two) young are born each year. The young, rather pale in colour, are born blind and remain with their parents for a year or even longer, the young of the previous year being included in a family group which also includes the newest litter.

Although gentle and easily tamed, Lesser Pandas do not usually thrive or survive in captivity.

*See 'European Mammals' *in this series*

Giant Panda (*below*)	Length, head and body	130 cm.
	Length, tail	12 cm.
	Weight	120 Kg.
Golden Takin (*above*)	Length, head and body	120 cm.
	Length, tail	10 cm.
	Horns up to	63 cm.

Giant Pandas are usually placed in the family *Procyonidae*, the Raccoons (order *Carnivora*), although some zoologists have considered them to be more closely related to the Bears. They are hardly carnivorous at all, their food consisting mostly of bamboo shoots, supplemented by some other plant food. Almost entirely ground-dwellers, they live in bamboo forests in mountainous areas on the borders of China and Tibet. Here they are well protected and, although rare, are not in such grave danger of extinction as are many better known Asian mammals. The Chinese authorities no longer permit the export of Giant Pandas.

Giant Pandas feed for up to twelve hours a day; they do not hibernate, the two cubs being born in January and weighing about four times as much as a Grizzly Bear* cub. Outside the breeding season they are solitary and rather silent. They were unknown to the western world until the eighteenth century and were not studied scientifically until the present century.

Herds of Golden Takin inhabit mountainous forests in the Shensi and Szechwan States of China. Discovered as recently as 1911, this race is somewhat rare, but other races are found in northern Burma, the Himalayas, Assam and Tibet. Takins, distant relations of the Musk Ox* (order *Artiodactyla*, family *Bovidae*), frequent dense bamboo thickets on which they feed and through which their bulk and shape enable them to make narrow paths, which are kept in continuous use.

The 'rut' takes place in July and August and the single calf is born in March or April. In winter the herds disperse and move to the valleys in small groups.

*See 'North American Mammals' *in this series*

Sika Deer (above)	Length, head and body	120 cm.
	Shoulder height	80 cm.
Raccoon Dog (below)	Length, head and body	52 cm.
	Length, tail	16 cm.

One of the largest families in the order *Artiodactyla* is the *Cervidae*, the Deer, and a large part of this family is made up of a sub-family known as *Cervinae*, the Asian and European Deer. Many members of this group occur in Asia, the Sika Deer being one which occurs in various forms in China, southern Asia, Formosa and Japan. Because of excessive hunting for food, pressure from expanding human development and because of the belief that the antlers possess some medicinal value, many of these races are almost extinct in their native habitats. But they have been established with great success in some European countries and in America, so the species may survive.

Sikas are usually spotted in summer but change to a drab winter coat. They are distinguishable at all times by the all-white rump and tail. Breeding and feeding habits are the same as for the larger Red Deer*, although Sika tend to form smaller herds or to be entirely solitary.

Another Asiatic mammal which has become established in Europe is the rather curious Raccoon Dog (order *Carnivora*, family *Canidae*). Called 'Raccoon' because of its facial markings, this is not a dog but a close relative of the Foxes. It occurs in Siberia, Manchuria, China and Japan and has recently wandered into Europe as far as eastern Germany and Sweden, via Russia.

The Raccoon Dog is unique among Canines in that in the northern part of its range it hibernates throughout the winter. It is nocturnal, omnivorous and more silent than most of this family.

*See 'European Mammals' *in this series*

Asiatic Bear (*above*)	Length, head and body	150 cm.
	Weight, up to	120 Kg.
Chinese Water Deer (*below*)	Length, head and body	90 cm.
	Length, tail	7 cm.

The Black Asiatic Bear (family *Ursidae*) has a wide range, extending from Afghanistan, through the Himalayas to China, Japan and Siberia. Thus it occupies the territory south of that of the Brown Bear* of Asia and Europe and north of that of the Sun Bears of southern Asia.

These Bears, which live in forests up to the tree limit in mountains, become immensely fat in autumn but do not hibernate in the strict sense of the word. Their winter 'sleep' is taken in a hollow tree, reputedly in a sitting position. Two cubs are born in this winter home and, as is common with all bears, are extremely small—about the size of rats.

In many respects they are similar to Brown Bears, but they are exceptionally aggressive and quite unafraid of man. They kill domestic stock and do considerable damage but are on the whole more vegetarian than most bears. They live in family parties and move about in single file, led by the father.

The little Chinese Water Deer (family *Cervidae*) is found in the marshes bordering the rivers of northern China. It has been introduced into England and France.

There are no antlers, but the upper canine teeth of the male are developed into quite long tusks. However, it does not rely much on these for defence as the Muntjac does, but protects itself by running for short distances or hiding in long grass or reeds.

Chinese Water Deer live on water plants. The young are born in litters of as many as five, an unusual feature in Deer, and these are kept in separate nests.

24   *See 'European Mammals' *in this series*

Tiger

Length, head and body   250 cm.
Length, tail   92 cm.
Weight, from   170 Kg.—270 Kg.

Tigers (order *Carnivora*, family *Felidae*) were originally inhabitants of northern Asia and still exist there in small numbers in such areas as Siberia, Manchuria and northern China. Over the centuries there has been a tendency for the species to move southward and westward and they are now established in India (but not Ceylon), Sumatra, Java and Malaya, as well as in Persia and the Caucasus. In some of these areas they are very scarce, and even in India, long considered to be their main stronghold, the Tiger is rapidly becoming a rare animal. To-day there are probably more Tigers in captivity than exist in the wild state. Because of persecution, destruction of their habitat and shortage of natural prey, the Tiger is facing extinction in the near future.

Usually nocturnal and solitary, Tigers hunt any mammal up to the size of Buffalo and young Elephant. Man-eating is more prevalent among Tigers than with any other cat. Prey is killed by a variety of methods—biting through the neck, striking with the fore-paw or throwing a moving animal so that it breaks its neck. A Tiger kills about thirty sizeable animals a year and seems to prefer meat which is 'high'.

The favoured habitat is reed beds or jungle, and Tigers prefer to live near water in which they immerse themselves during hot weather. Two to four cubs are born at varying times of the year, but the whole of a litter rarely survives.

Tigers in the northern part of the range tend to be larger and paler and have longer fur. Southern Tigers are smaller and brightly coloured.

Clouded Leopard (*above*)	Length, head and body	100 cm.
	Length, tail	90 cm.
	Weight	20 Kg.
Temminck's Golden Cat (*below*)	Length, head and body	76 cm.
	Length, tail	48 cm.

There are more species of cats in Asia than anywhere else in the world. Because they live in remote areas and are nocturnal, many of them are rarely seen and not generally known. A great many species, hunted for fur and because they prey upon domestic stock or poultry, are becoming rare.

The Clouded Leopard is found from India and China southward to Borneo, Sumatra and Java. It is an inhabitant of dense jungle, living for most of the time in large forest trees. In spite of its size it is unexpectedly light and is thus able to hunt for birds and small mammals along quite thin branches. It will also kill small domestic animals and, like Leopards, dogs. It is said to be more easily tamed and more gentle than others of this family and is believed to produce from two to four cubs in each litter.

Temminck's Golden Cat has a close relative in the African Golden Cat, and they are quite hard to tell apart. This beautiful animal occurs from Tibet, through India and Burma to south-east Asia, Malaya and Sumatra. Not much is known of its natural history and it occupies varying habitats. It is said to produce two kittens to a litter.

Both these animals belong to the order *Carnivora* and to the family *Felidae*. The other small cats (genus *Felis*) of Asia, as opposed to the Great Cats (genus *Panthera*) include the Marbled Cat, Bornean Red Cat, Flat-headed Cat, Rusty Spotted Cat, Chinese Cat, Leopard Cat, Fishing Cat and Pallas' Cat. The Caracal, Lynx and Jungle Cat also occur in Asia.

Ounce (Snow Leopard)

Length, head and body   135 cm.
Length, tail   92 cm.

The Ounce is included among the Big Cats (genus *Panthera* and family *Felidae*) and inhabits the highlands of central Asia. It ranges from Persia, where there are very few, to Turkestan, Kashmir and Tibet, thence to the Altai Mountains and Mongolia. Much of these areas is hardly populated and, as Ounces live in such isolated parts of the world and are chiefly nocturnal, they are very rarely seen. Although living high in the mountains, Ounces, being carnivores, have to go where their prey can be found. This consists of Markhor, Tahr and other Asiatic mountain goats. Hares, Gazelle, Deer and Pheasants are taken in the lower-lying areas to which Ounces descend in the winter. Some domestic stock is also taken.

Prey is stalked, but the final distance is covered in one enormous leap, Ounces having been credited with jumps of sixteen metres long.

As it is one of the Big Cats, the Ounce roars—though very rarely. Unlike the tropical members of this family, breeding takes place at fixed times of the year and the two to four cubs are born in April after a gestation period of some ninety-three days. This is similar to that of the Leopard and Jaguar, and compares with the sixty-three days of the European Wild Cat.

Unfortunately the beautiful fur of this animal attracts trappers and hunters. The winter coat is much thicker and longer than that of summer, and in cold weather the long furry tail is wound round the Ounce as it sleeps in its den among the rocks.

Malayan Tapir
(below)

Length, head and body	*200 cm.*
Length, tail	*7.5 cm.*
Shoulder height	*91.5 cm.*

Gaur *(above)*

Length, head and body	*300 cm.*
Length, tail	*85 cm.*
Shoulder height	*220 cm.*
Weight More than one metric ton.	
Cows much smaller	

Tapirs belong to the order *Perissodactyla*, the odd-toed, hoofed mammals, and to the family *Tapiridae*. There are four species, three in south and central America and one in Asia. The similarity of these species supports the theory that at one time many species crossed the land bridge between Asia and America.

Malayan Tapirs inhabit Burma, Indo-China, Sumatra and Malaya. They have three small hooves on each foot and differ from American Tapirs chiefly in the colour pattern. They favour a habitat of forest with an adequate supply of water, for they are expert swimmers and can stay submerged for some time. They are good climbers of hilly country, creating tracks which follow the safest and most practicable routes. They are strictly vegetarian and are most active at night.

Young Tapirs, usually born singly, are dark skinned with white and yellow spots and stripes which last for the first six months of their lives.

Gaur (order *Artiodactyla*, the even-toed hoofed mammals) belong to the family *Bovidae*. This massive animal is the largest of all the cattle, of which there are many species, both wild and domestic, in Asia. It is found (nowadays in decreasing numbers) throughout the Indian peninsula, Burma, Indo-China and into Malaya, where it is known as the Seladang. In north-east India it is known as the Mithun.

Gaur are both grazers and browsers, feeding in the early morning and in the evening and retiring to thick cover during the day. Like all cattle they live in small herds and, when threatened, can be dangerous. Calves are born singly in August or September.

Anoa (*below right*)

Length, head and body	150 cm.
Length, tail	25 cm.

Babirusa (*above left*)

Length, head and body	100 cm.
Length, tail	30 cm.
Weight	90 Kg.

Both these animals are found only in the Celebes or in the neighbouring small islands.

The Anoa, a buffalo in miniature, is the smallest member of the world's cattle. It inhabits wooded, well-watered areas, usually in the highlands. In spite of being a somewhat shy animal it has been greatly over-hunted, partly for its flesh and very thick hide, and partly for so-called 'sport'. The immense increase in human population and development, common thoughout much of south-east Asia, has also had the effect of reducing its numbers. Both the Anoa and its near relative the Tamarau (in the Philippines) are in danger of extinction. But if properly protected and farmed they could provide a much needed food for human use.

This rather aggressive animal feeds chiefly on cane shoots and produces a single calf.

The Babirusa is a member of the Pig family, the *Suidae* (order *Artiodactyla*). The astonishing tusks spring from both jaws, the upper ones piercing through the skin on top of the muzzle. They apparently serve no useful purpose and are developed in the male only. These almost hairless pigs inhabit the banks of streams or lakes, spending much time in the water and even swimming in the sea to reach small islands.

Babirusas are much hunted for food and are often domesticated. They are becoming rarer. The young, born in litters of two only (which is few for this family) are not striped as other piglets are.

Other Asian pigs include the Javan Pig and Bornean Pig; and the Wild Boar, known both in Europe* and Africa, also occurs.

34   *See 'European Mammals' in this series

Indian Rhinoceros

Length, head and body	
up to	400 cm.
Length, tail	60 cm.
Shoulder height up to	200 cm.
Weight up to	4000 Kg.
Length of horn up to	60 cm.

There are three species of Rhinoceros in Asia; all of them are rare. Two of them, the Javan and Sumatran species are virtually extinct. The third, and by far the largest species, is the Great Indian Rhinoceros (order *Perissodactyla*, family *Rhinocerotidae*) which inhabits parts of north-east India and Nepal, mostly in game sanctuaries. There are probably no more than 625 of them left in the wild. The smaller two-horned Sumatran Rhino numbers about 170, and of the Javan Rhino, found now only in the Udjong Kulon Reserve in Java, there are at most only forty.

The numbers of Rhino have decreased because they have been grossly over-hunted, not only by 'sportsmen' with highly efficient modern rifles, but also by poachers who kill the Rhino for its horn. Some eastern people believe that this has magical, medicinal properties.

Indian Rhinos are solitary, inhabiting areas of tall grass or jungle near rivers and swamps in which they love to wallow. They differ from the species found in Africa* in having great folds of skin dividing up their huge bodies. This skin is hairless, but the single 'horn' is actually composed of hairs compressed together. Grass and reeds provide their food, and they are nearly always accompanied by Cattle Egrets which feed on their ticks or on insects disturbed by the Rhino as it grazes.

Single calves, suckled by the mother for two years, are born between February and April. Indian Rhinos live for fifty years or more. They are not very intelligent and their sense of sight is poor, but the senses of smell and hearing are good.

*See 'African Mammals' *in this series*

Indian Elephant

Length, head, body and trunk up to	640 cm.
Length, tail up to	150 cm.
Shoulder height up to	300 cm.
Weight, about	5000 Kg.

Indian Elephants (order *Proboscidea*, family *Elephantidae*) have been domesticated for centuries, trained to use their immense strength and intelligence in transport work and in shifting heavy articles such as timber.

In the wild they are found in small herds, always led by an old female. A variety of habitats is favoured, from thick jungle to grassland; but an extensive water supply is essential for bathing and wallowing. Wild Indian Elephants are found in the southern half of India and in Ceylon, which has a distinct but dwindling race of its own, and in Burma, Siam, Malaya and Sumatra. They are exclusively vegetarian, being both browsers and grazers, and the average adult Elephant eats about 225 Kg. of food a day.

The Asiatic Elephant differs from the African* species in being generally smaller, with smaller ears and a flatter back. There are also differences in the number of ribs and nails and in the tip of the trunk which, in the Indian Elephant, has only one moveable 'finger', while that of the African has two.

Unless molested, wild Indian Elephants are inoffensive. The calves are usually produced singly, although twins are not unknown. There is no definite breeding season and the gestation period is as much as 640 days, sometimes less. Indian Elephants are fully-grown at twenty-five and can live for about seventy years.

The Elephant's supposed powers of memory are probably no better than those of any other domesticated animal of equal intelligence, such as a dog or horse. But they possess an infinite capacity to learn and are subjected to training over a lengthy period.

*See 'African Mammals' *in this series*

Wild Bactrian Camel (*above*)	Length, head and body	300 cm.
	Length, tail	50 cm.
	Shoulder height	200 cm.
Kulan (Asiatic Wild Ass) (*below*)	Length, head and body up to	220 cm.
	Length, tail	45 cm.
	Shoulder height up to	150 cm.

The Gobi Desert is the home of the Wild Bactrian Camel, of which a few still remain in two groups along isolated river valleys and on the high plateaux of western Mongolia. The world population of this wild species is about five hundred head.

The Wild Bactrian Camel (order *Artiodactyla*, family *Camelidae*) differs from the domesticated form in being longer in the leg, with smaller humps, and in having a shorter coat. The domestic form is found throughout China and Mongolia, in Siberia and in many other parts of Asia. They are essentially draught animals and are not much used for riding. Like other Camels they supply wool and hide, meat, milk, sinews and bones for man's use.

Bactrian Camels have feet suitable for moving easily over sand or snow. Closeable nostrils and thick lashes protect them from sandstorms and blizzards, and they can stand great extremes of temperature. Principally vegetarian, they will eat anything if sufficiently hungry. Fat is stored in the humps, but Camels do not store water and need it just as much as other desert mammals do. Calves are born singly and are fully-grown in five years.

Wild Asses (order *Perissodactyla*, family *Equidae*) occur from Mongolia westward to Tibet, Afghanistan and Persia. There are three forms, all occupying desert habitats.

The Kulan is found in Mongolia, the larger Kiang in Tibet, and the pale-coloured Onager ('Ghor-Khar' in India) in Persia. All are shy, fast-moving animals which form herds, often in company with Gazelles, and they produce single foals. All forms of Wild Ass are rare and are decreasing in numbers.

Axis Deer (Chital)	Length, head and body	150 cm.
(above)	Length, tail	25 cm.
	Shoulder height	80 cm.

Chousingha (below)	Length, head and body	100 cm.
	Length, tail	12 cm.
	Shoulder height	60 cm.

Among the deer of Europe and Asia (sub-family *Cervinae*) the Axis Deer is perhaps the most beautiful. This deer belongs to the same family (*Cervidae*) as the Fallow Deer and Red Deer*. The males carry wide, simple antlers, and the summer coat of both sexes is spotted. There are three species, the chief of which is found in India and Ceylon, while another occurs in the Philippines; the third species, much shorter in the leg, is known as the Hog Deer and occurs in India and Indo-China.

Axis Deer inhabit open forest and are usually diurnal, grazing in large herds composed of both sexes. According to locality, they breed at various times of the year and produce two young (sometimes three). They do well in captivity and have been introduced into many countries of the world as park deer.

Other Asian members of this family are the Sambar, Thamin, Hangul, Shou, and many others, some of them becoming increasingly rare.

Although several species of Gazelle occur in Asia, there are few species of Antelope. The most curious of them is the Chousingha or Four-horned Antelope, the only one in the world so equipped. It occurs in India in open forest and, unlike other Antelopes, is a solitary animal which dashes for cover at the slightest sign of danger. Females do not carry horns, but both sexes have a peculiar jerky action on minute rounded hooves.

From one to three young are born and, like all Asian *Artiodactyls*, this occurs after the rainy season is ended and when the new grass has started to grow.

*See 'European Mammals' *in this series*

Leopard (*top*)	Length, head and body	130 cm.
	Length, tail	90 cm.
	Weight	90 Kg.
Blackbuck (*below left*)	Length, head and body	120 cm.
	Length, tail	17 cm.
	Shoulder height	80 cm.
Nilgai (*below right*)	Length, head and body	200 cm.
	Length, tail	50 cm.
	Shoulder height	135 cm.

Leopards have a most extensive range throughout Asia, from the Middle East to China and Korea and from the Himalayas to Indonesia. Although varying slightly according to locality, Asian Leopards are otherwise the same as those found in Africa and are described in 'African Mammals' in this series. Chinese Leopards are the largest, with long, beautifully marked fur, and Black Leopards occur chiefly in the tropics.

The Blackbuck (family *Bovidae*, order *Artiodactyla*) is one of the fastest animals in the world, able to outrun even the Cheetah*. It is found in West Pakistan and through most of India. This is an animal of open grassland and is a grazer, active during the day. Unlike most other members of this family the males are coloured differently from the females, old males being particularly dark. Only the males carry horns, and a single buck will have a small group of about twenty females. Two or three young are born, and the life span is about fifteen years.

The Nilgai occurs in central India in forest land or jungle. This large Antelope is both grazer and browser, the bulls being usually solitary while the cows, which are paler in colour and hornless, form small herds which include their calves, usually born in pairs. During the breeding season the bulls fight, as other Antelope do, but apparently choose to do so on their knees.

The chief enemies of the Nilgai are the Tiger and Leopard; it is not much sought by man as a trophy or as food, being regarded by the Indians as a relative of the sacred Cow.

*See 'African Mammals' *in this series*

Wild Yak *above*)

Length, head and body	310 cm.
Length, tail	73 cm.
Shoulder height	190 cm.

Chiru (Tibetan Antelope) *(below)*

Length, head and body	135 cm.
Length, tail	10 cm.
Shoulder height	80 cm.

The family *Bovidae* contains some truly impressive animals, not least of which is the Wild Yak. The appearance of the bulls in particular is made even more impressive by the long, coarse hair with its fringes and thick undercoat. Females are much smaller, but generally Wild Yaks are about twice the size of the more familiar domestic Yaks which the Tibetans have kept for centuries for meat, milk, hide and as pack animals.

Although protected by the Chinese Government, the Wild Yak is in grave danger of extermination. Modern rifles, often of insufficient calibre to be lethal to such a large animal, but nevertheless capable of causing serious wounds, are now available to poachers.

Wild Yaks live above 4500 metres elevation and below 6000 metres in the desolate parts of the Tibetan Plateau. They produce single calves and live on whatever vegetation their habitat provides.

Chiru (order *Artiodactyla*, family *Bovidae*) are related to the Saiga Antelope* and share, in modified form, the same 'inflated' nose and special features. As mammals they are placed somewhere between the Gazelles and the Goat-antelopes. They occupy plateau areas up to 5500 metres in Tibet.

Very shy and wary, Chiru excavate depressions in snow or soil in which they shelter. They can trot for long periods at a speed which outpaces Wolves or Lynxes, and the spectacular horns carried by the male can inflict terrible wounds. This frequently happens during fights between the bucks during the 'rut' in November. Calves are born in May and form separate herds with their mothers.

Chiru have not been kept in captivity and little is known about them.

*See 'European Mammals' *in this series*

Asiatic Buffalo (*above*)	Length, head and body	300 cm.
	Length, tail	100 cm.
	Shoulder height	180 cm.
	Horns up to	120 cm.
	Weight up to	815 Kg.
Barasingha (*below*)	Length, head and body	180 cm.
	Length, tail	12 cm.
	Shoulder height	130 cm.
	Antlers up to	104 cm.

The tribe *Bovini* (the cattle) of the family *Bovidae* has many species in Asia which have been domesticated. These include the Gayal, Zebu and Domestic Buffalo. Other wild species include, besides those previously mentioned in this book, the Banteng of south Asia and Indonesia, and the rare Kouprey, discovered only in 1936 in Indo-China. The various pressures of human development are making it increasingly difficult for them to survive, and the Kouprey, for instance, may already have become extinct as a result of the wars in Indo-China.

The Asiatic Buffalo has the longest horns of any member of this family. It is fully capable of dealing with attacks by Tigers and frequently kills Domestic Buffalo bulls. The Asiatic Buffalo occurs in Assam, Nepal and Bengal and lives sometimes in herds and sometimes solitary, in habitats of long grass and swamp. It is frequently caked with mud, in which it wallows to keep off the attentions of insects. It lives on water plants and grass and produces one or two calves.

If molested these animals can be extremely dangerous, as can the Domestic Buffalo to those humans it does not know.

Barasingha are beautiful deer, of the same family as Red Deer*, which live in swamps in north and central India and in Nepal. Stags and hinds live in separate herds and the hinds each produce one fawn a year. The species is declining in numbers owing to the invasion of its habitat by domestic cattle.

'Barasingha' means 'twelve-pointer', indicative of the number of 'tines' (points) grown on the antlers.

*See 'European Mammals' in this series

Pangolin (*below*)	Length, head and body	30-80 cm.
	Length, tail	35-80 cm.
Bushy-tailed Cloud Rat (*above*)	Length, head and body	35 cm.
	Length, tail	38 cm.

The extraordinary Pangolin, covered with horny scales and toothless, is placed in an order, *Pholidota*, and a family, *Manidae*, by itself. There are seven species, four of which occur in Africa and three in Asia. They inhabit open grassland or thick forest, and are found in India and Ceylon, China, Formosa, Malaya, throughout Indonesia to Bali, Borneo and the Philippines. They were once classed with the Anteaters, for their chief item of food consists of ants and termites. They gather these on a sticky tongue so long that the base of it is anchored on the pelvis—the bone to which the hind legs are attached.

To defend themselves Pangolins roll into a tight ball, and such is their strength that it is impossible to 'unwind' them. They also eject a foul-smelling liquid from special glands. They are nocturnal.

Some Pangolins live in trees and others in burrows on the ground, but all climb well. A single youngster is produced whose scales become hard in about two days.

The Bushy-tailed Cloud Rat is one of several kinds of rats peculiar to the Philippines and neighbouring islands. And yet it is a member of the same huge family of rodents, the *Muridae*, to which the ordinary House Mouse* belongs. Its long, bushy tail and fur are unique features in this family, of which there are many species in Asia.

These rats are arboreal and nocturnal and utter a peculiar, shrill cry. They feed on pine bark and various fruits. Related species occur in New Guinea and Australia, thus forming a mammal link between the two continents.

*See 'European Mammals' *in this series*

INDEX